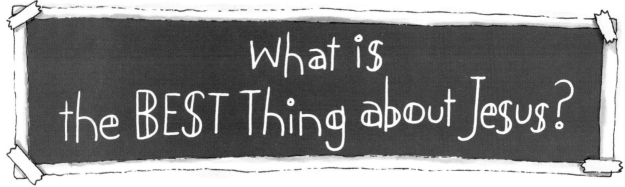

What is the BEST Thing about Jesus?

This book is narrated by Christine . . .

. . . but her voice is really the voice of Christine Harder Tangvald, author of more than 50 children's books. With her enthusiastic eye-level, heart-level style that kids really understand, Christine communicates to kids how much she cares. She's a mother and grandmother and has worked with children for more than 20 years. Christine and her husband, Roald, live in Spokane, Washington.

*Dedicated to every parent, teacher, grandparent, and friend
who communicates to a single child (even in a small way)
the GIFT of LIFE — salvation through faith in our Lord and
Savior, Jesus Christ. Such important work! Thank you, each one!
— C.H.T.*

The Standard Publishing Company, Cincinnati, Ohio
A division of Standex International Corporation
Text © 1994 by Christine Harder Tangvald
Illustrations © 1994 by The Standard Publishing Company
All rights reserved.
Printed in the United States of America
01 00 99 98 97 96 95 94   5 4 3 2 1

Library of Congress Catalog Card Number 94-10001
ISBN 0-7847-0164-4
Cataloging-in-Publication data available

Edited by Diane Stortz
Designed by Coleen Davis

Scripture from the *International Children's Bible, New Century Version.*
© 1986, 1989 by Word Publishing, Dallas, Texas 75039.
Used by permission.

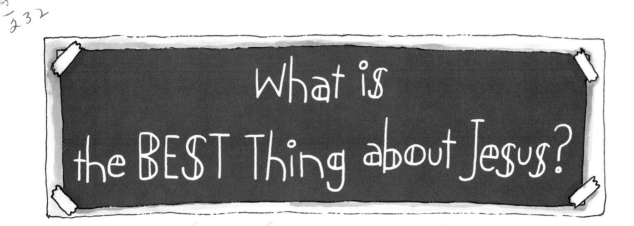

What is the BEST Thing about Jesus?

written by Christine Harder Tangvald
illustrated by Kathy Couri

STANDARD
PUBLISHING
Cincinnati, Ohio

Oh! Hello there! How *are* you?
I am *so* glad to see you, because I need your help!

My name is Christine, and I have a problem, a big, *big* problem.
You see, I am making a book about the BEST thing about Jesus.
But there are *so* many wonderful things about Jesus
that it is *hard* to decide which is BEST.

Will you please
help me choose?
Will you please
help me finish
my *special* book?

You *will?* Oh, good!
First, let's go through
this book together.

(That will be fun!)

And then you can help me choose which is the BEST thing about Jesus.
OK? Are you ready? Here we *go!*

Maybe the BEST thing about Jesus is his *birthday!*
Did *you* know that Christmas is Jesus' birthday?

It is!
Long, long ago in a little stable
in Bethlehem, baby Jesus was born.

Mary and Joseph were there, too.
And on that holy night,
in a burst of bright, bright light,
angels sang to shepherds in the fields!

"Wow!" said the shepherds. "We must find this holy baby!"

And they did.
They found baby Jesus in a manger,
and they worshiped him.

I wish *I* could have been there.

I wish *I* could have heard the angels sing.

I wish *I* could have been with the shepherds and seen baby Jesus, too . . .

don't *you?*

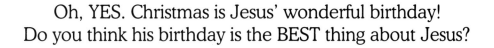

Oh, YES. Christmas is Jesus' wonderful birthday!
Do you think his birthday is the BEST thing about Jesus?

But Jesus didn't stay a baby.
Oh, *no*.

Jesus grew . . .   and *grew* . . .   and GREW!

And then Jesus began
to teach and preach
about his Father, God.

Maybe *that's* the BEST thing about Jesus —
that he is God's very own Son!

He is, you know. Jesus is God's *only* Son.
And do you know what God said about Jesus?
God looked down from high above and said — right out loud —

"This is my Son and I love him.
I am very pleased with him."

And God's Spirit came down on Jesus like a dove.

Wow!
Do you think the BEST thing about Jesus
is that he is God's own Son?

But maybe all the wonderful things Jesus did are the BEST thing about him.

Did you know that Jesus walked across a lake . . . right on top of the water?

He *did!*
It was a *miracle!*

And one time Jesus healed a blind man!
"I can see! I can see!" said the man.

Wow!
It was *another* miracle!

Another time, Jesus fed more than
5,000 *hungry* people with only five
loaves of bread and two small fish!
     (I wonder how he did *that*.)
And once there was a terrible storm.

The wind *whooshed*
     and the waves *swooshed*.
"Help! Help!" cried Jesus' friends.
"Stop! Be still!" said Jesus to the storm.
And the storm stopped . . . *just* like *that!*

Do you know any other exciting stories about Jesus?

Oh, YES!
I like all the wonderful things Jesus did.
But are they the BEST thing about him?

Maybe his wise, wise words are the BEST thing about Jesus.

Jesus is smart, you know,
really smart,
because he is God's own Son.
His wise, wise words are written for us to read in the Bible.

Here are some of my favorites.
Have *you* heard any of these wise, wise words before?

"I will be with you always."
Matthew 28:20

"Love the Lord God with all your heart."
Matthew 22:37

"LOVE EACH OTHER AS I HAVE LOVED YOU."
John 15:12

"Do for other people the same things you want them to do for you."
Matthew 7:12

"He who has seen me has seen the Father."
John 14:9

"For God so loved the world that he gave his only Son."
John 3:16

Wow!

Do you know any other wise, wise words Jesus said?

Oh, YES. I like Jesus' wise, wise words.
But are his words
the BEST thing about Jesus?

And I like ALL the wonderful names of

Jesus

How many names can you find on these two pages?

don't *you?*

Sometimes Jesus is called the

Good Shepherd

(That's because he loves and cares for his people like a shepherd loves and cares for his sheep.)

Sometimes Jesus is called

Immanuel

(That means "God with us.")

Sometimes Jesus is called the

LAMB of GOD

or

SAVIOR

or the

LIGHT of The WORLD

or

Christ the LORD

And here are four more names of Jesus.

Wonderful Counselor,

Powerful God,

Father who Lives forever,

Prince of Peace

AND

Jesus is KinG of KinGs
AnD
LORD of LORDS !

Wow!
Jesus has a *lot* of exciting names, doesn't he?
How many did you count?
Which one is *your* favorite?

But are his wonderful names the BEST thing about Jesus?

Maybe God's amazing plan is the BEST thing about Jesus.

Do you know about
God's amazing plan — for you?

Well, listen to *this.*

When Jesus is our very own Savior,
then God forgives all
the bad things we think
and all the bad things we do!

God loves us so much
that he sent his own Son,
Jesus, to be our Savior.

Because of Jesus, our sins are washed away!

Whoosh, swoosh! They're gone!

It's all a part of God's AMAZING plan.

You see, it's true
that Jesus did die
for our sins.

But Jesus *did not*
stay dead.
        Oh, no,
        he did NOT!

On the third day, God made Jesus ALIVE again!

It was *amazing!* . . .

"He's alive!" said all his friends.
"Jesus is alive!"

"Wow!" they said.

They were *so* happy.
And so am I!
     I'm happy that Jesus is alive — right now!
But that's not all . . .

(*Do you know what happened next?*)

God took Jesus right up, *up*, UP . . .

      through a cloud . . .

            into a glorious place called HEAVEN!

And someday *we* can go to HEAVEN, too!
Because when we have faith in Jesus,
he *promises* us life with him . . .

                    forever!

And Jesus is coming *again*.
Isn't that GREAT!
Everyone will see him! (I can't *wait!*)

Then *all* of Jesus' friends will go
back to HEAVEN with him, *forever!*

Yay! Hooray!
What a great day
that will be!

Hmmm . . .

Maybe God's amazing plan *is* the BEST thing about Jesus.

Maybe the BEST thing about Jesus
is that he is my very own friend!
He is, you know!
He is *your* friend too, right now!

And Jesus is a *special* friend
because he will never, *ever* leave.
Never. EVER!

You know, friends love and care about one another.
And being friends with Jesus feels nice.
    Very, *very* nice.
Jesus said, "Let the children come to me!"
    Isn't it great that God sent such a special
    friend to love and care for me and you?

It makes me want to say,

Jesus, Jesus, I love you!
    And I know you love me too.
I want you to be my friend
    and give me love that has no end!
And Jesus, be my Savior too,
    'cause Jesus, Jesus, I love you!

Oh, my!
Being friends with Jesus *does* feel nice, doesn't it?
    Nice and *safe*.
Is *that* the BEST thing about Jesus?

And since we are good friends with Jesus, we can talk to him!
Did you know that?

Oh, YES! Jesus likes it when we talk to him.
Talking to Jesus is called *prayer.*

It's *easy* to pray. You just say,

"Hi, Jesus! It's me, _____ *(say your name).*"

And then you talk about anything you want to!
And you can talk to Jesus anytime, from any place.
And he listens.
Jesus *always* listens when we pray.

Talking to Jesus is *important!*
Hey! Do you have something you want to talk to Jesus about — right now?
Go ahead. I'll wait for you.

"Hi, Jesus! It's me, _____ *(say your name).*
Here is something I want to tell you, Jesus.

_____

_____

_____ . "

Amen! (That means, "The end.")

I always feel better after I talk with Jesus, don't you?

Maybe the BEST thing about Jesus
is that we can talk to him anytime,
anyplace, about anything!

Wow!

Oh, *my!*
I think Jesus is WONDERFUL, don't you?
I love Jesus *so much* that I want
to tell everyone else about him too!
I want to *shout,*

"Hey you guys! I think Jesus terrific colossal, incredibly, fantastically wonderful!"

Don't *you?*

...IS Super,

So, now you can see what a *big* problem I have.
How can I possibly choose
which is the BEST thing about Jesus?
Will you please help me now?
Will you please help me choose?
You will? Oh, *thank you!*

Do you think the BEST thing about Jesus is his *birthday?*

Is it that
Jesus is
God's own
Son?

Could it
be the
wonderful
names
of Jesus?

Is it the *wonderful
things* he did,
or his *wise,
wise words*
we can read
in the Bible?

Maybe the
BEST thing
about Jesus
is God's
amazing plan!

Do you think the BEST thing could be
that Jesus is our very own *friend* and *Savior,*
and that he *loves* and *cares for us,* right now and *forever?*

Or is it that we can *talk with him* whenever we want to?

Can you think of any other
wonderful things about
Jesus?

WELL,

what have you decided?

What did
you choose?

What do *you* think
is the BEST thing
about Jesus?

Can you go back
and point to it with your finger?
Or say it out loud, right now?

Or write your answer here.
I think the best thing about Jesus is

_____

_____

_____ .

Wow!

That is a good thing about
Jesus that you chose.
Thank you so much
for helping me finish
my book.

I simply couldn't have
done it without you!

Well, this has been fun, hasn't it,
working on my book together?
    It is sad to say good-bye to you.
    I will miss you.

        Hey, I know what!
Maybe we can read through *this* book
together again sometime.
    I'd like that.
    I'd like it a *lot.*

Just remember this — Jesus loves you,
        today, tomorrow,
        and *always!* (And so do I!)

Good-bye, my special friend!

Much love,
from Christine